Food Coloring Book

PSYCHEDELIC STRESS-RELIEVING FOOD

A Coloring Book For Adults

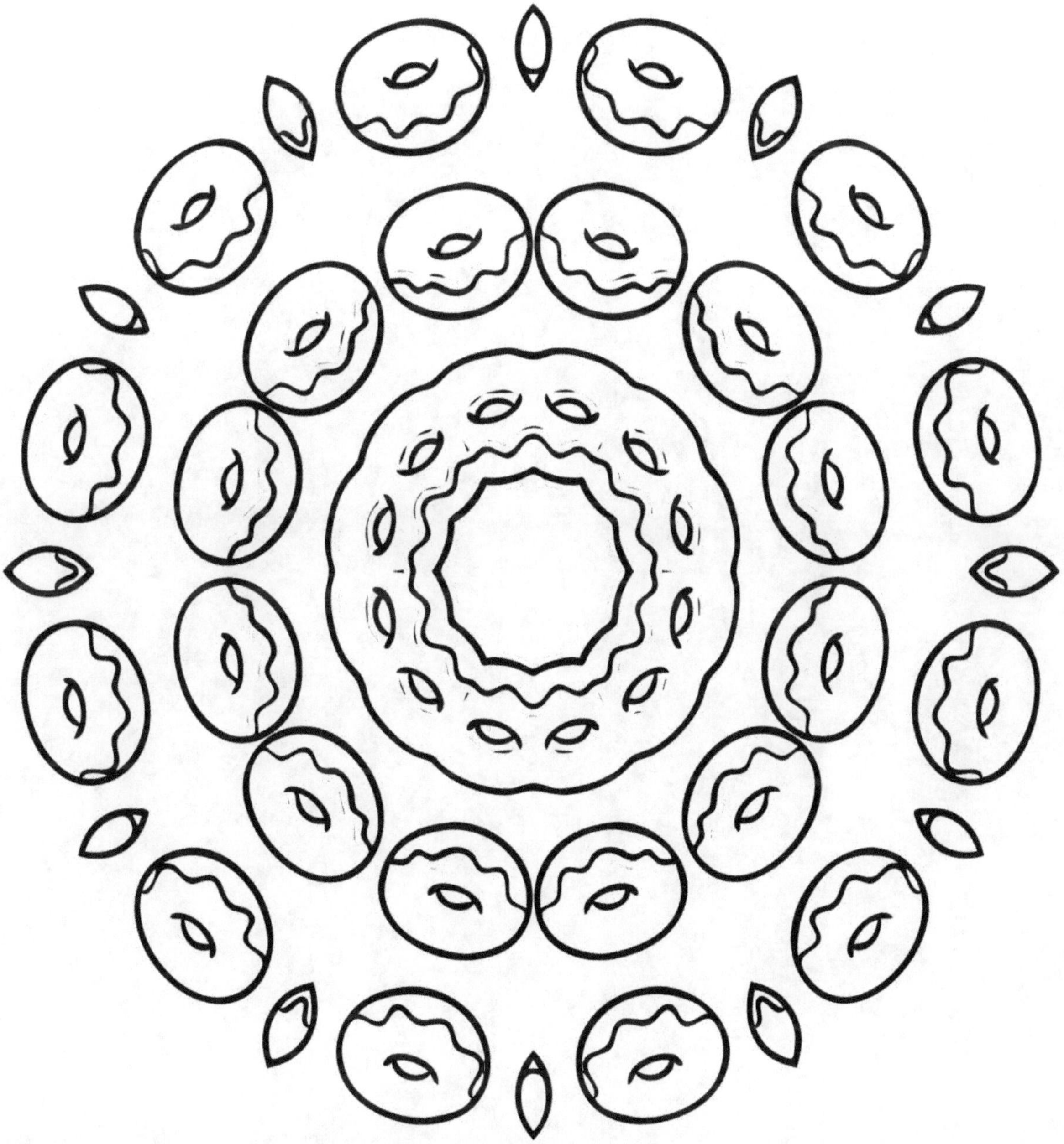

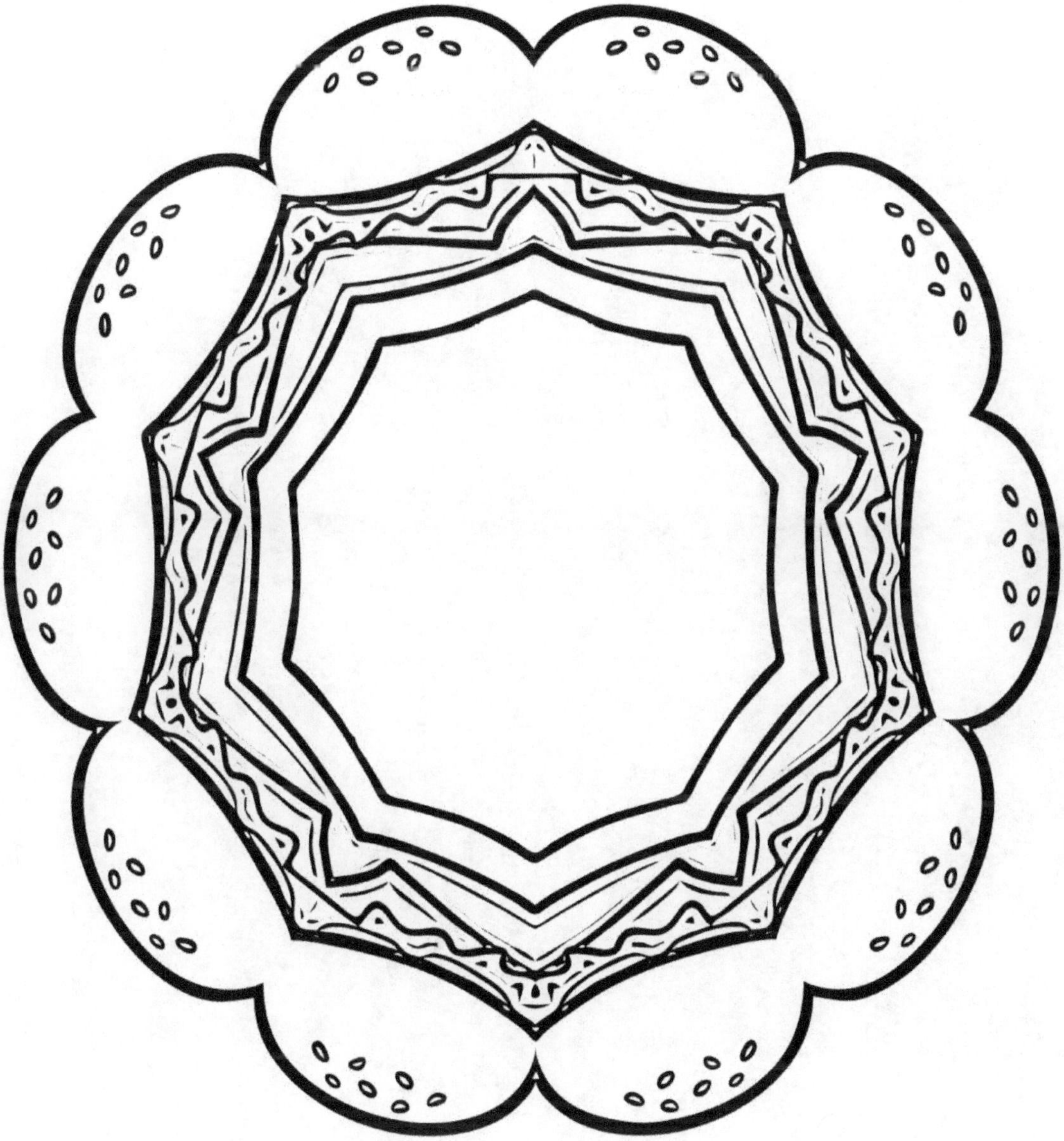

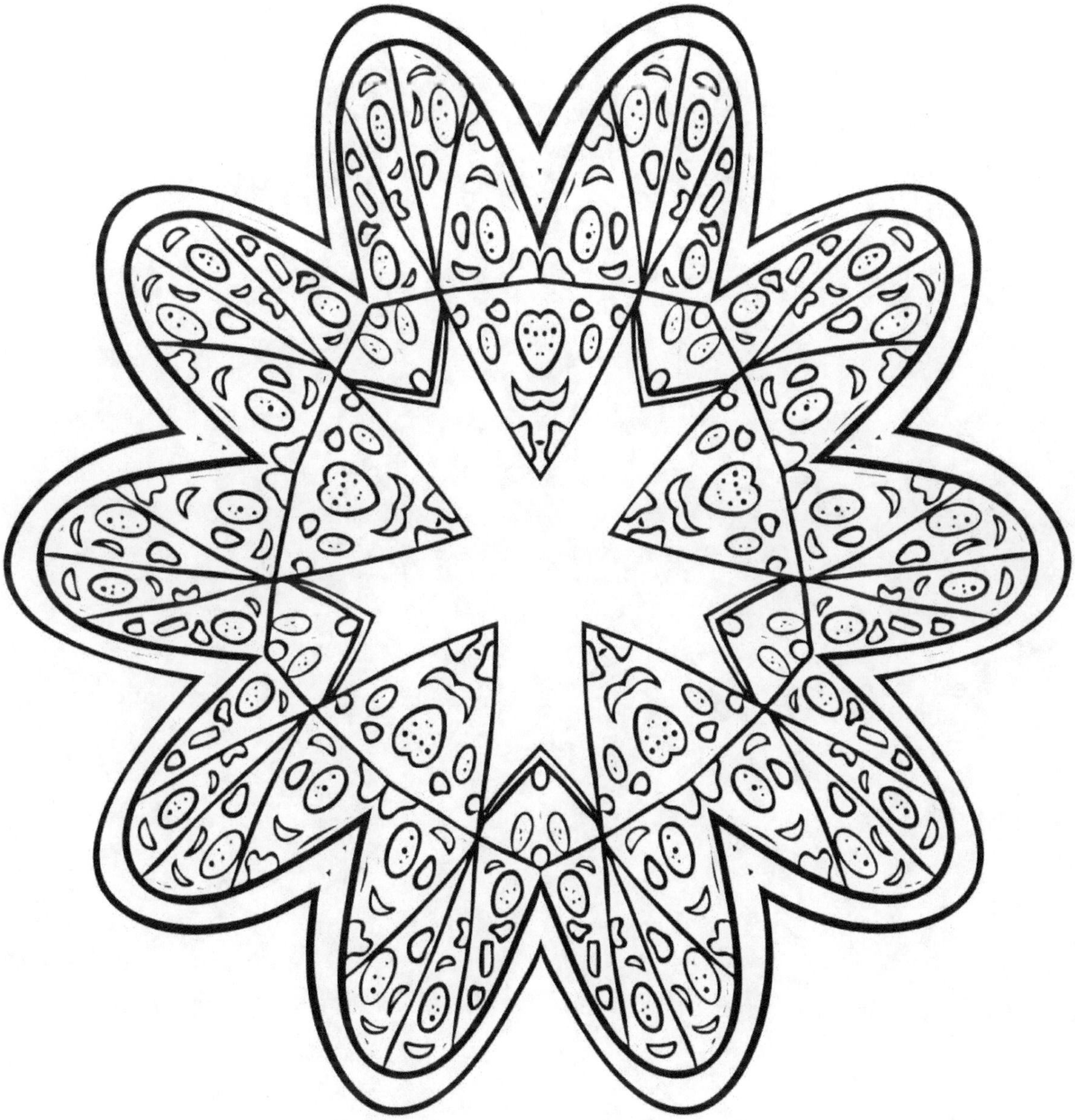

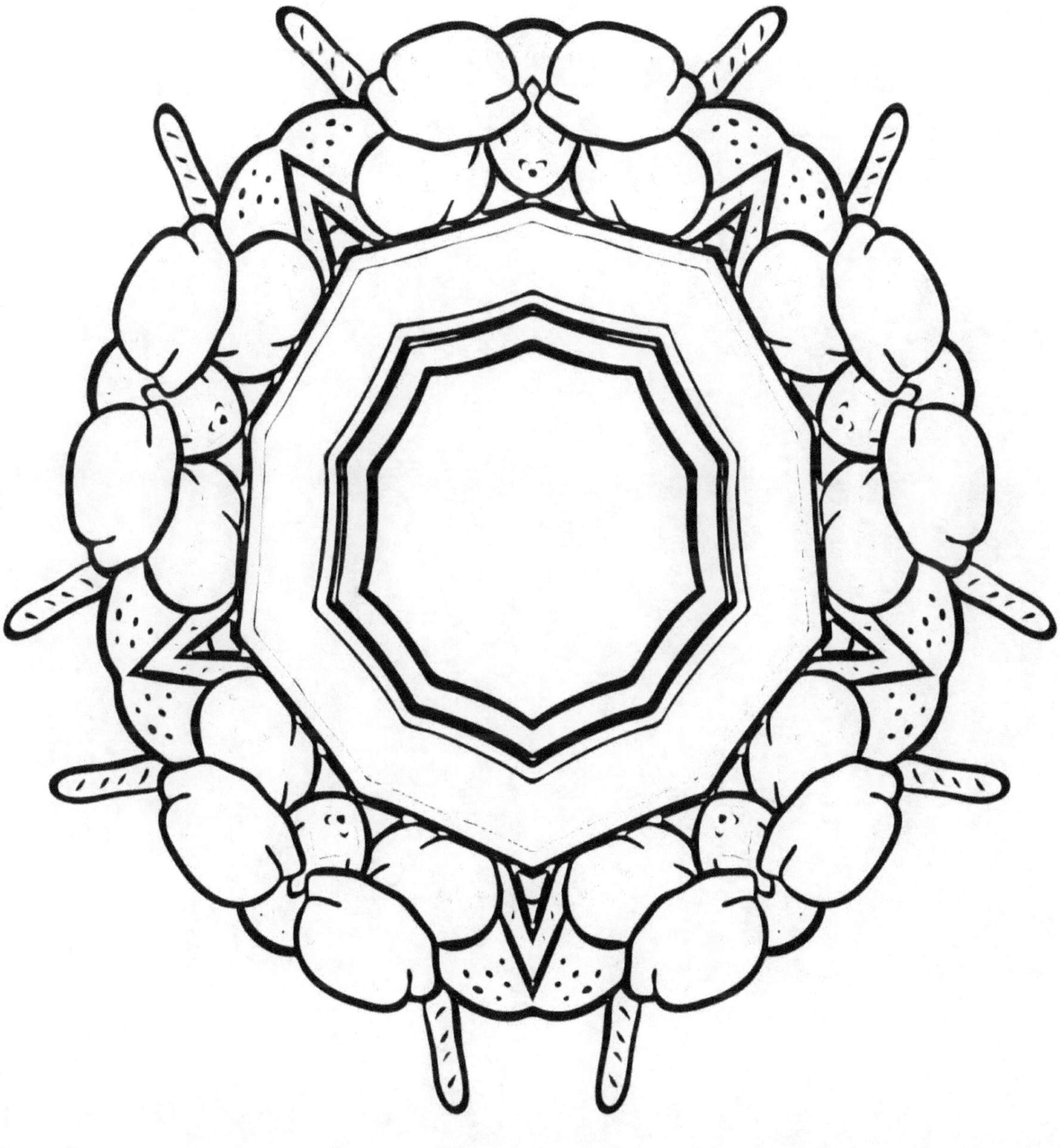

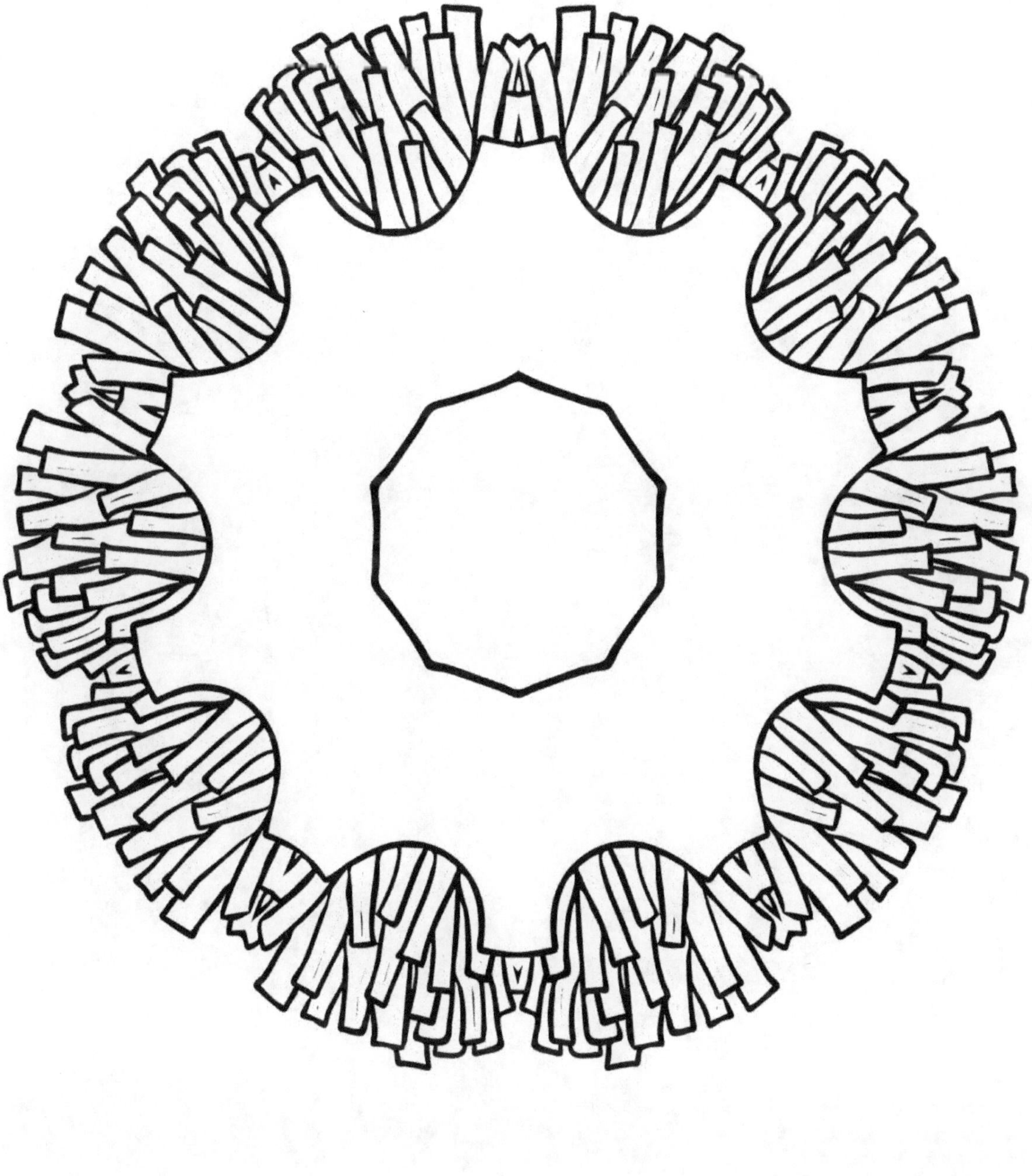

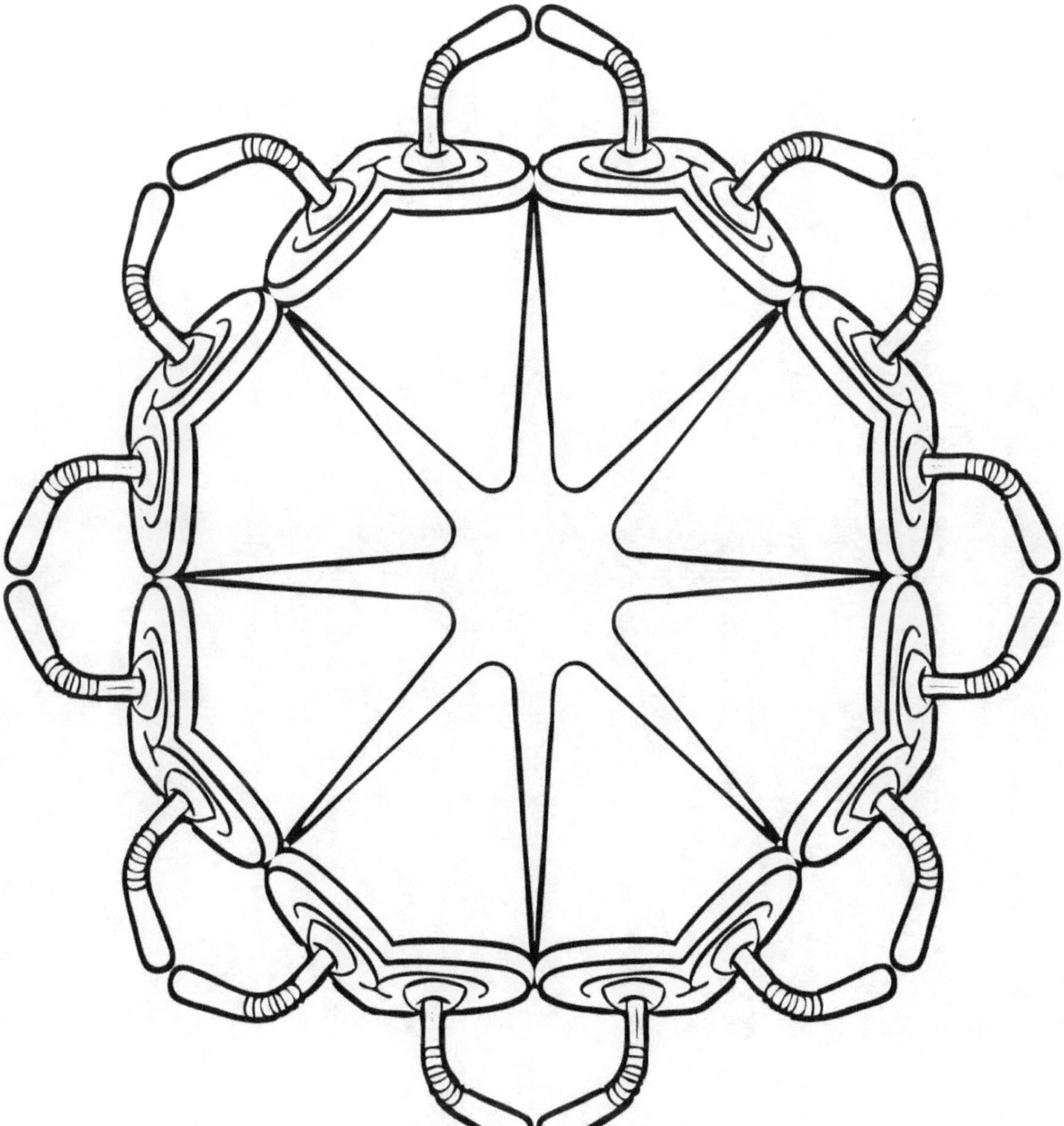

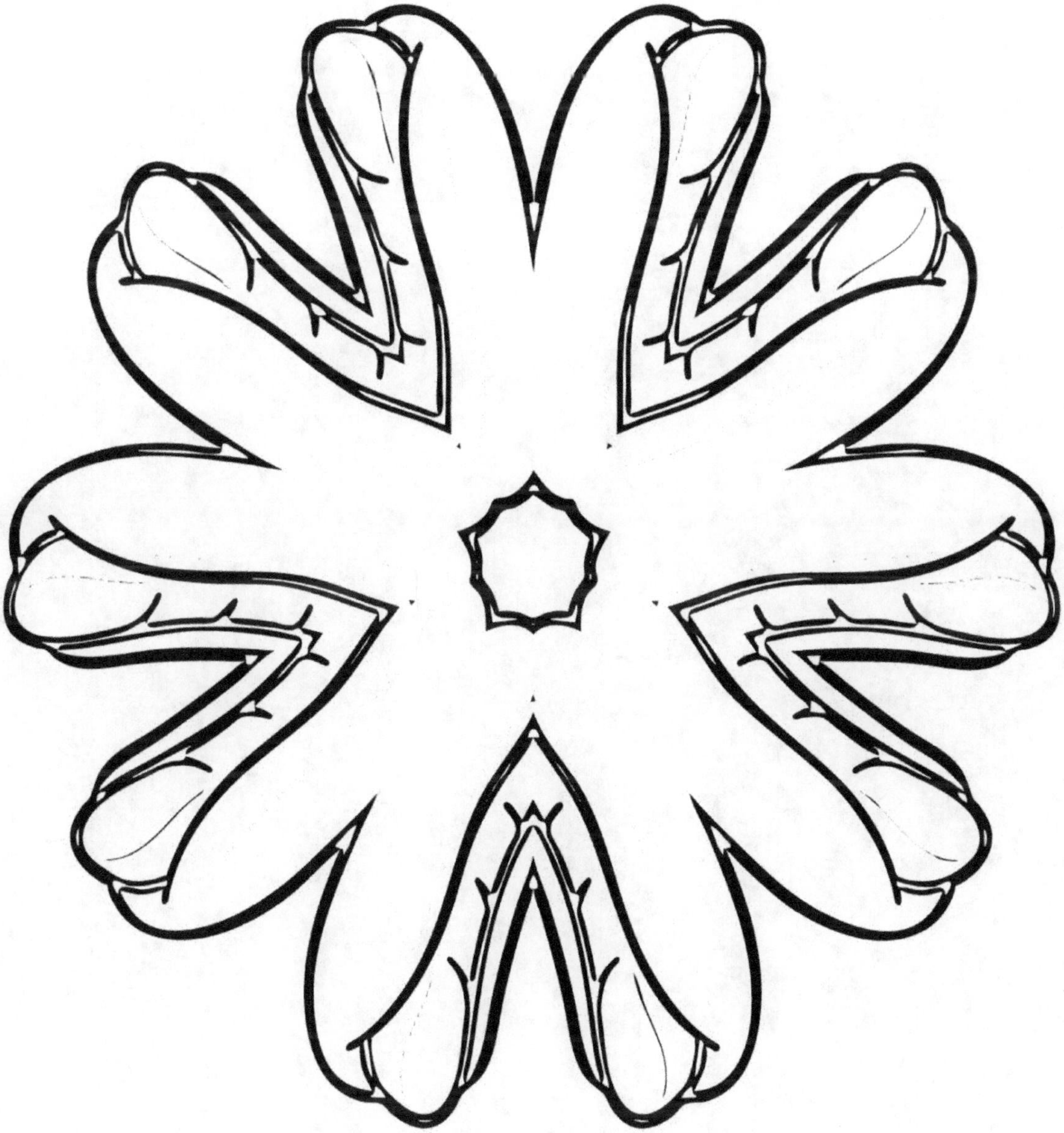

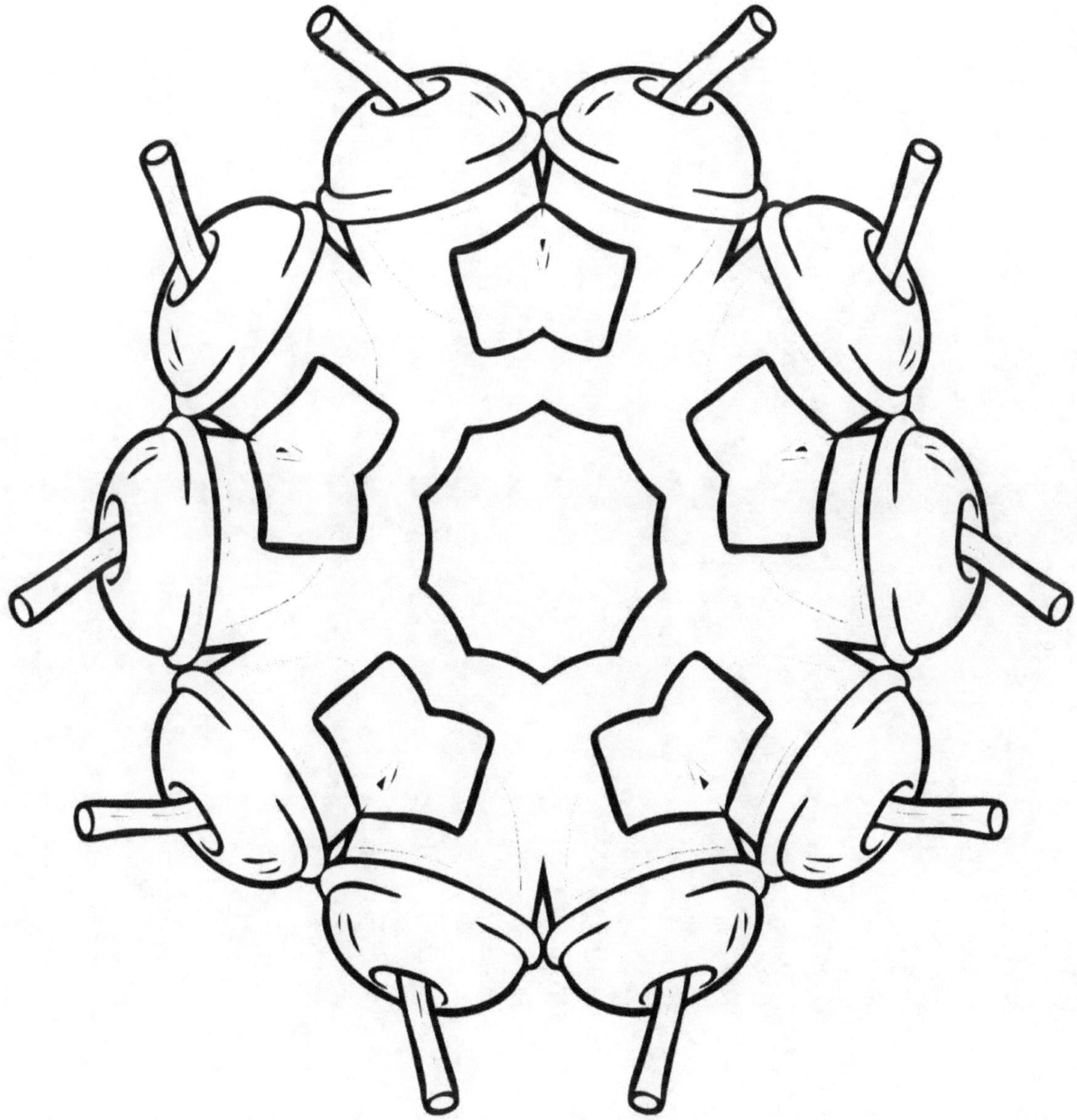

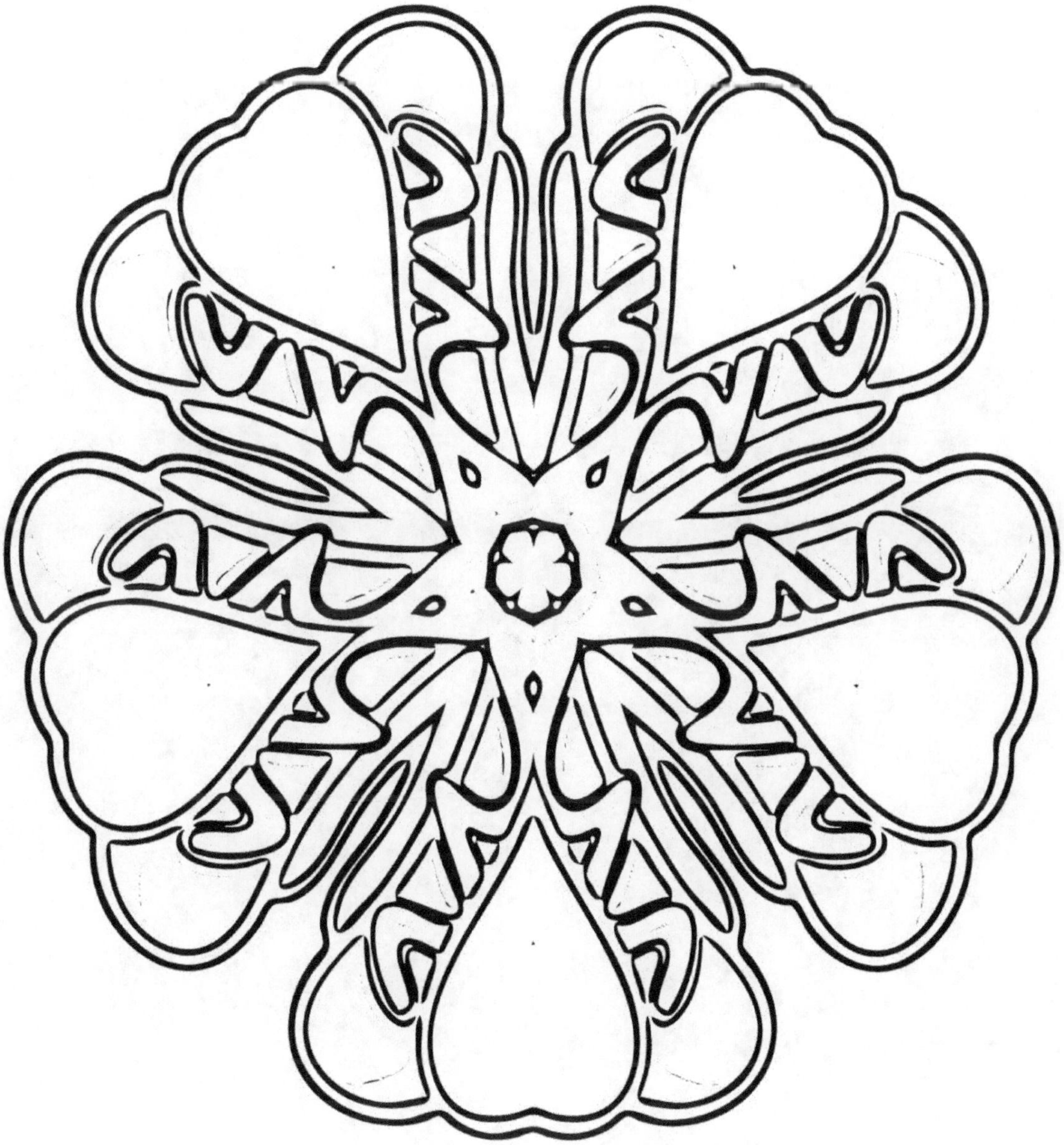

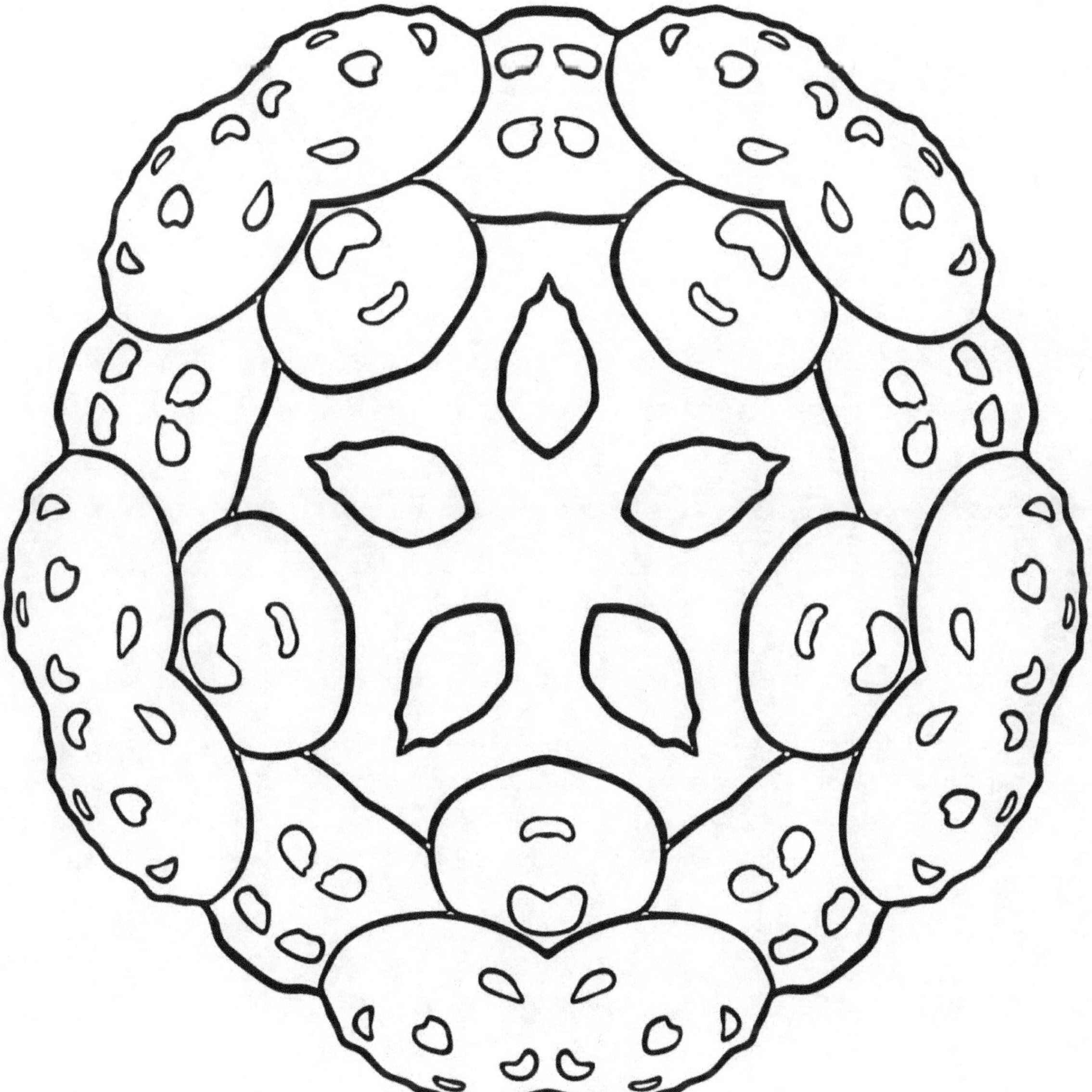

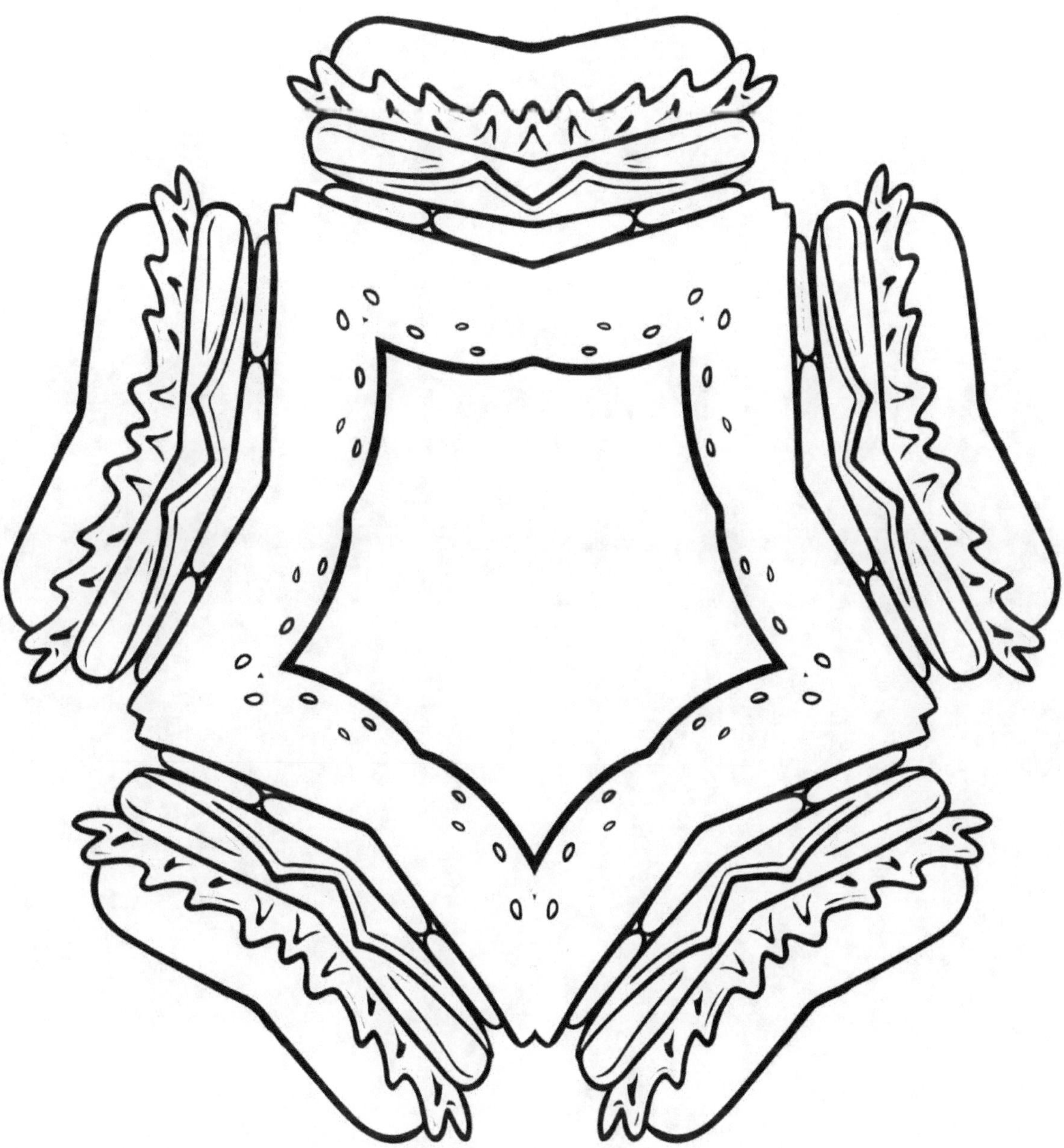

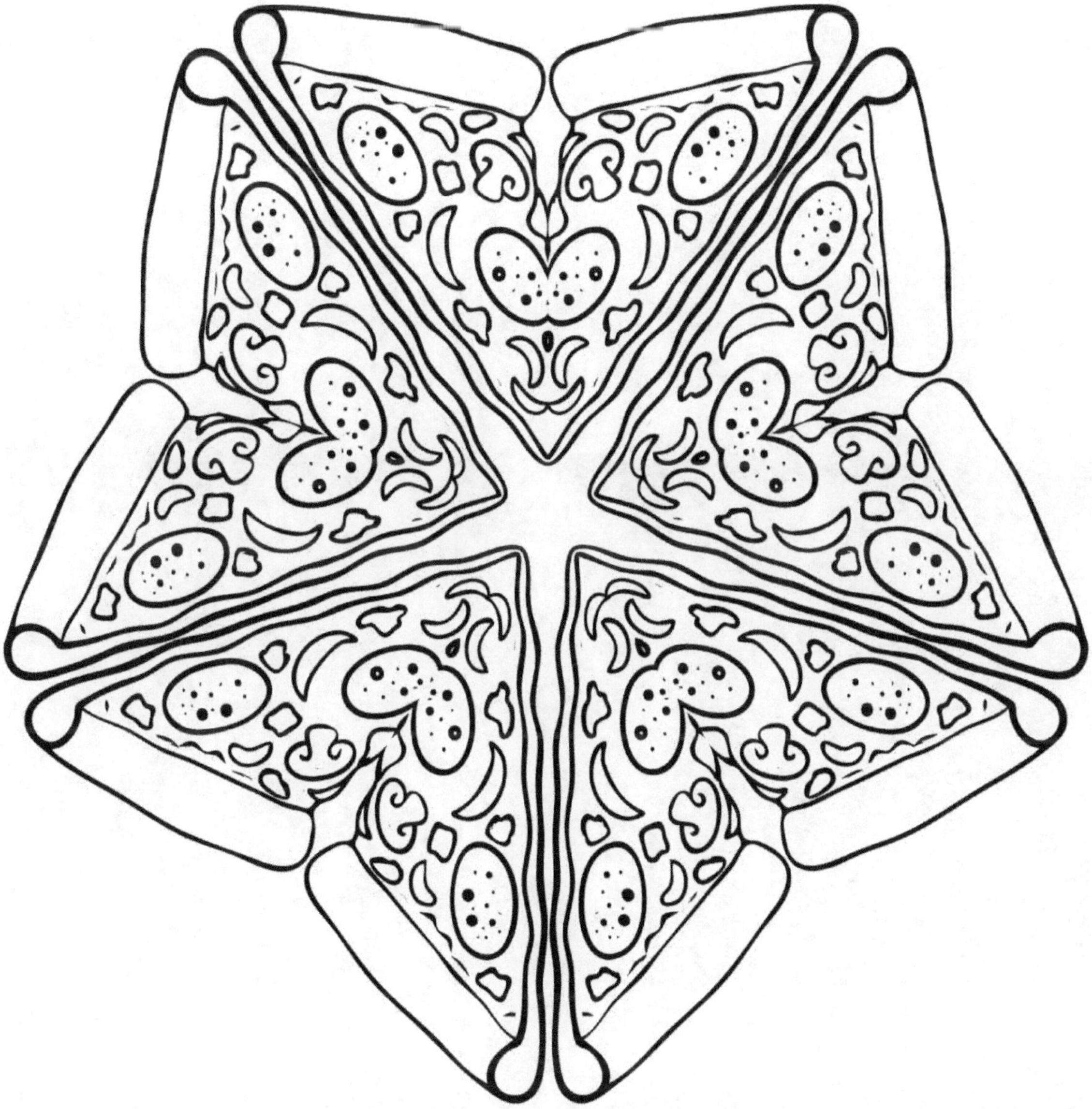

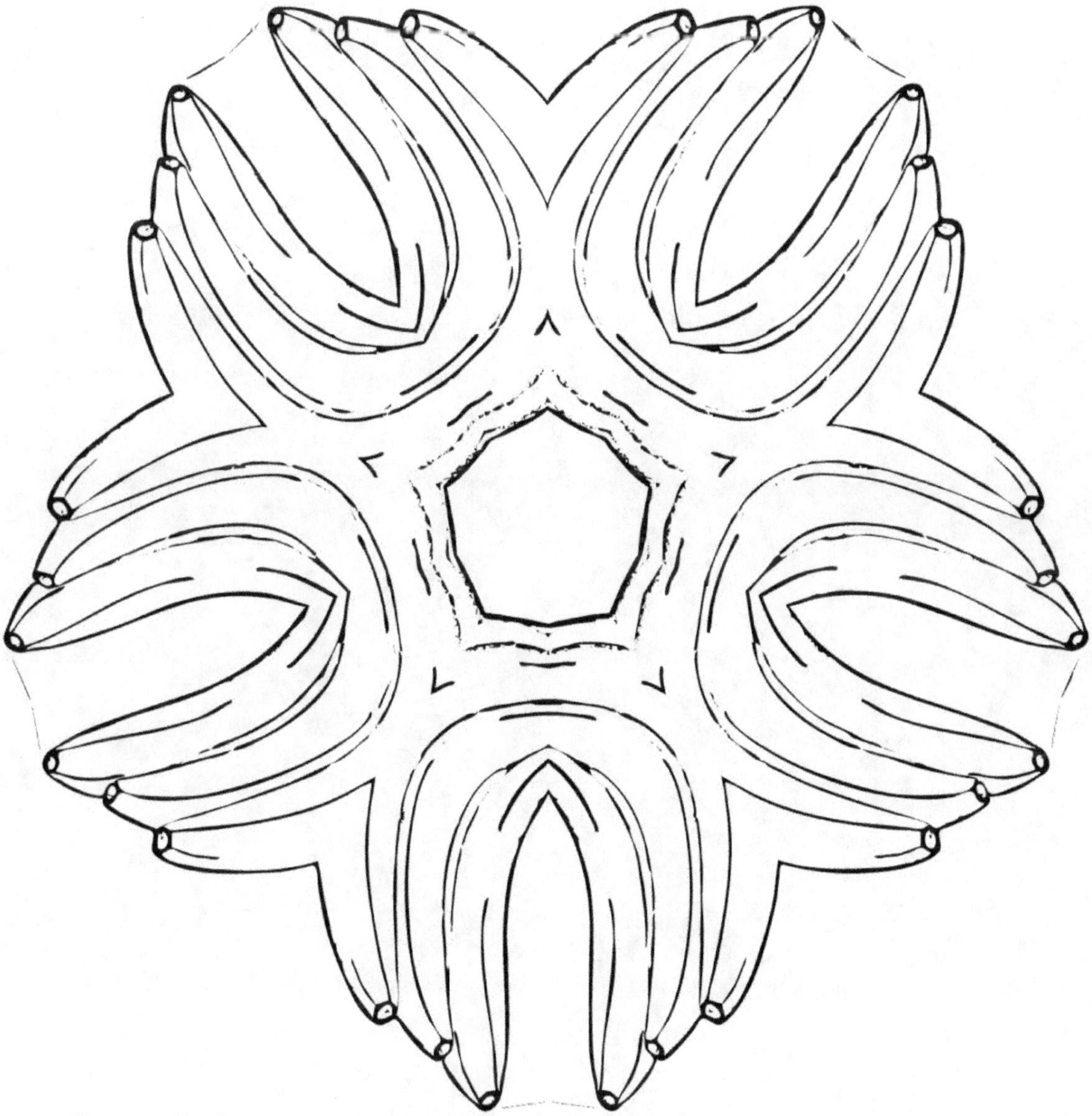

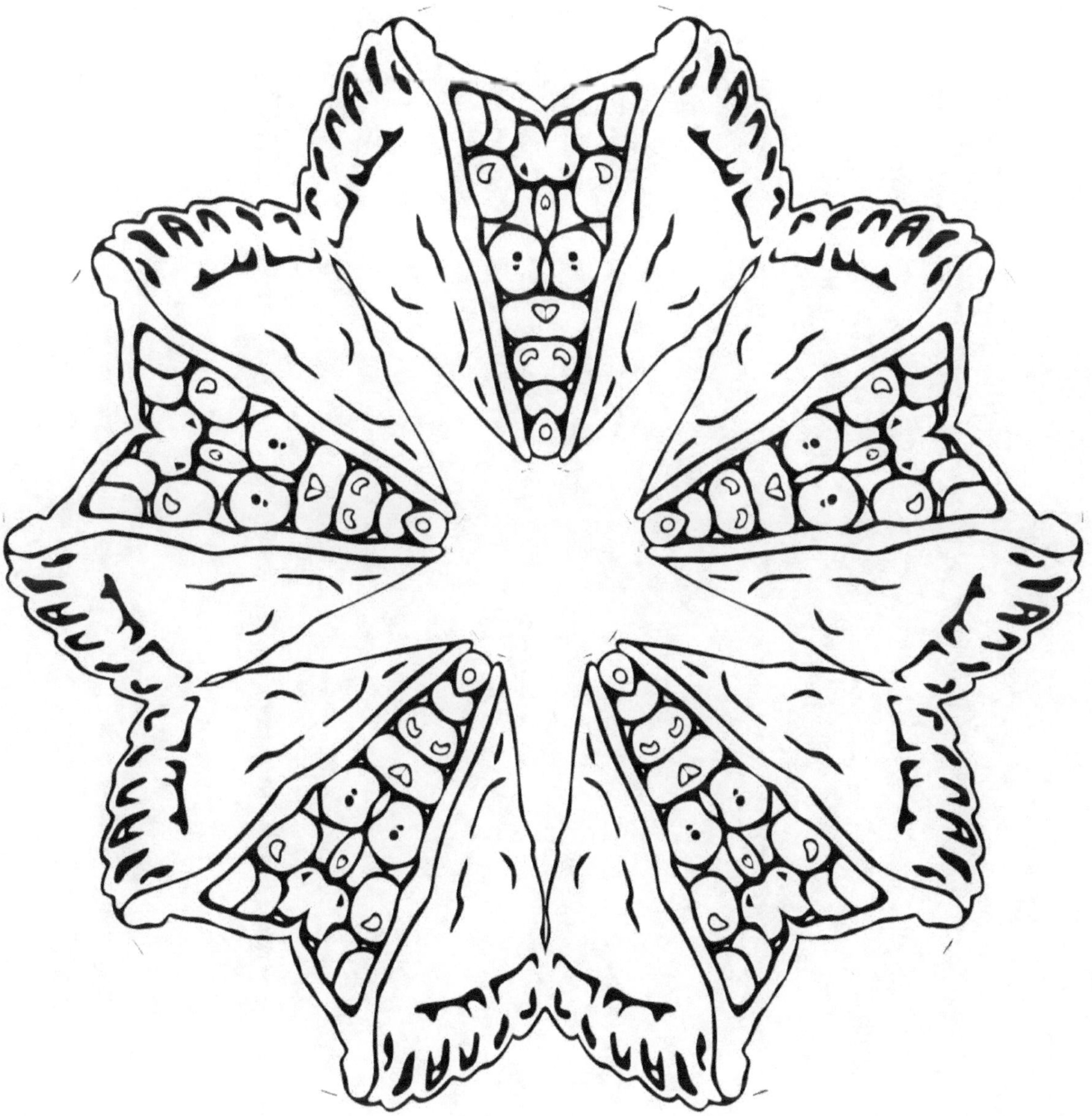

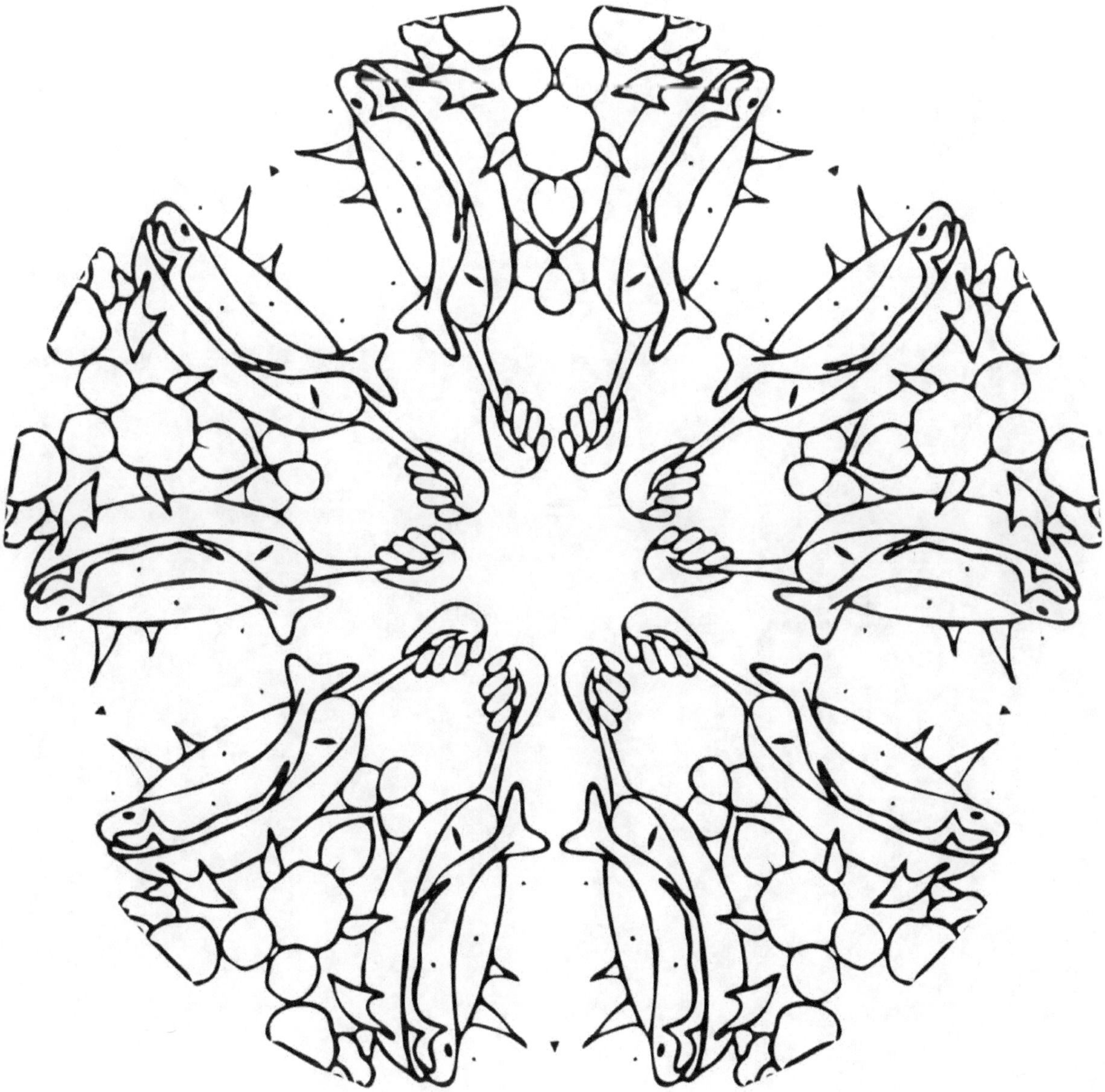

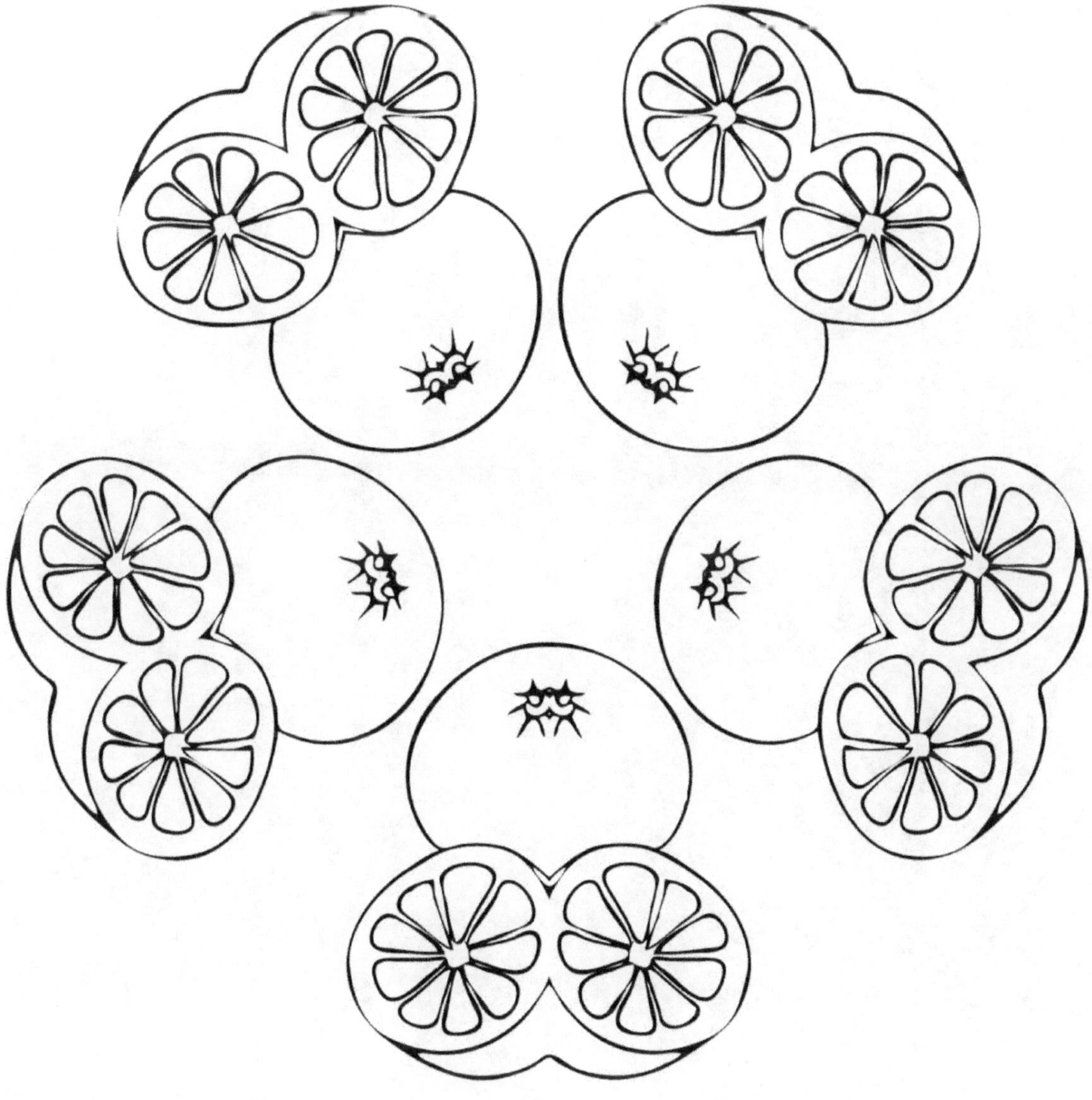

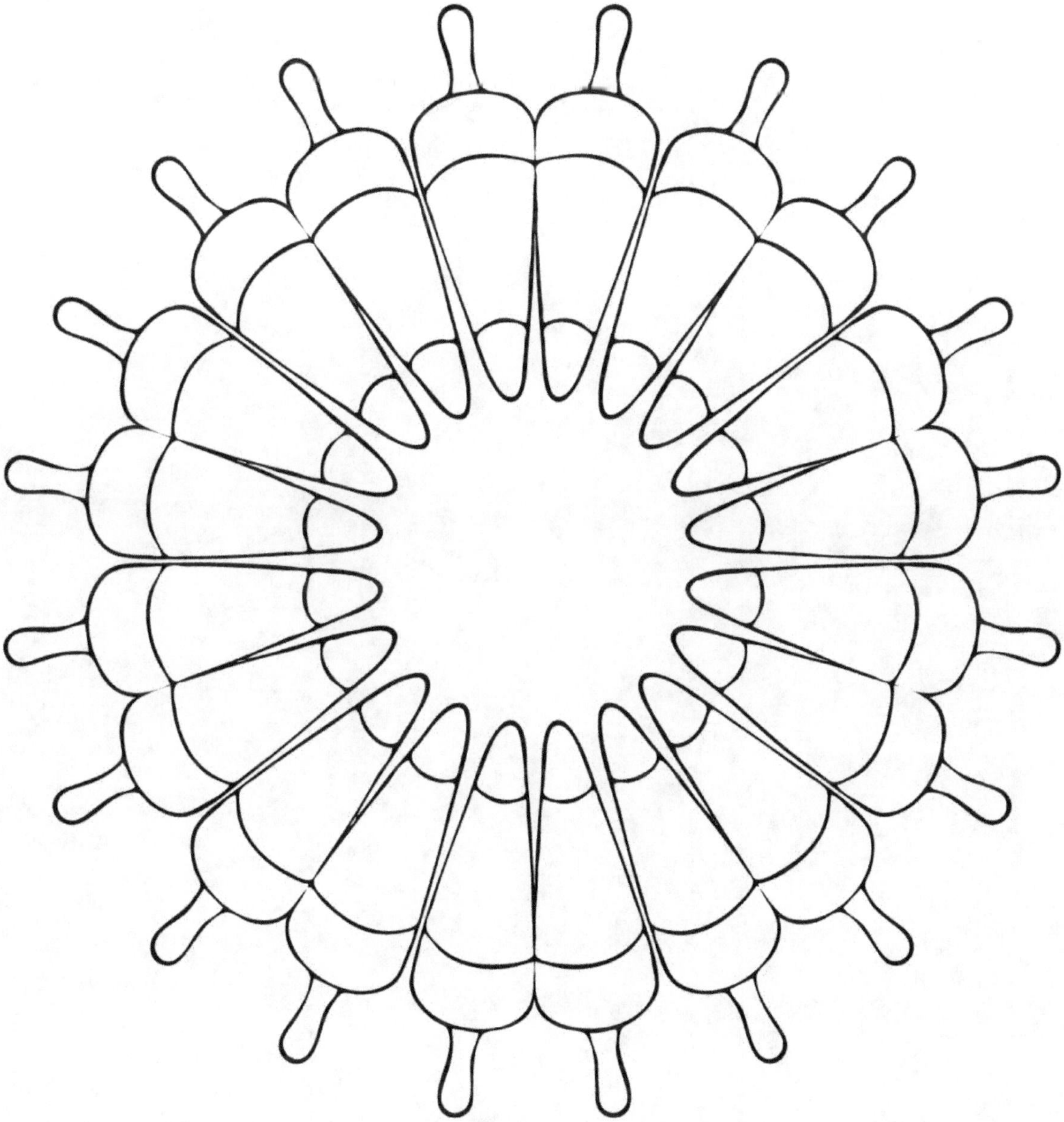

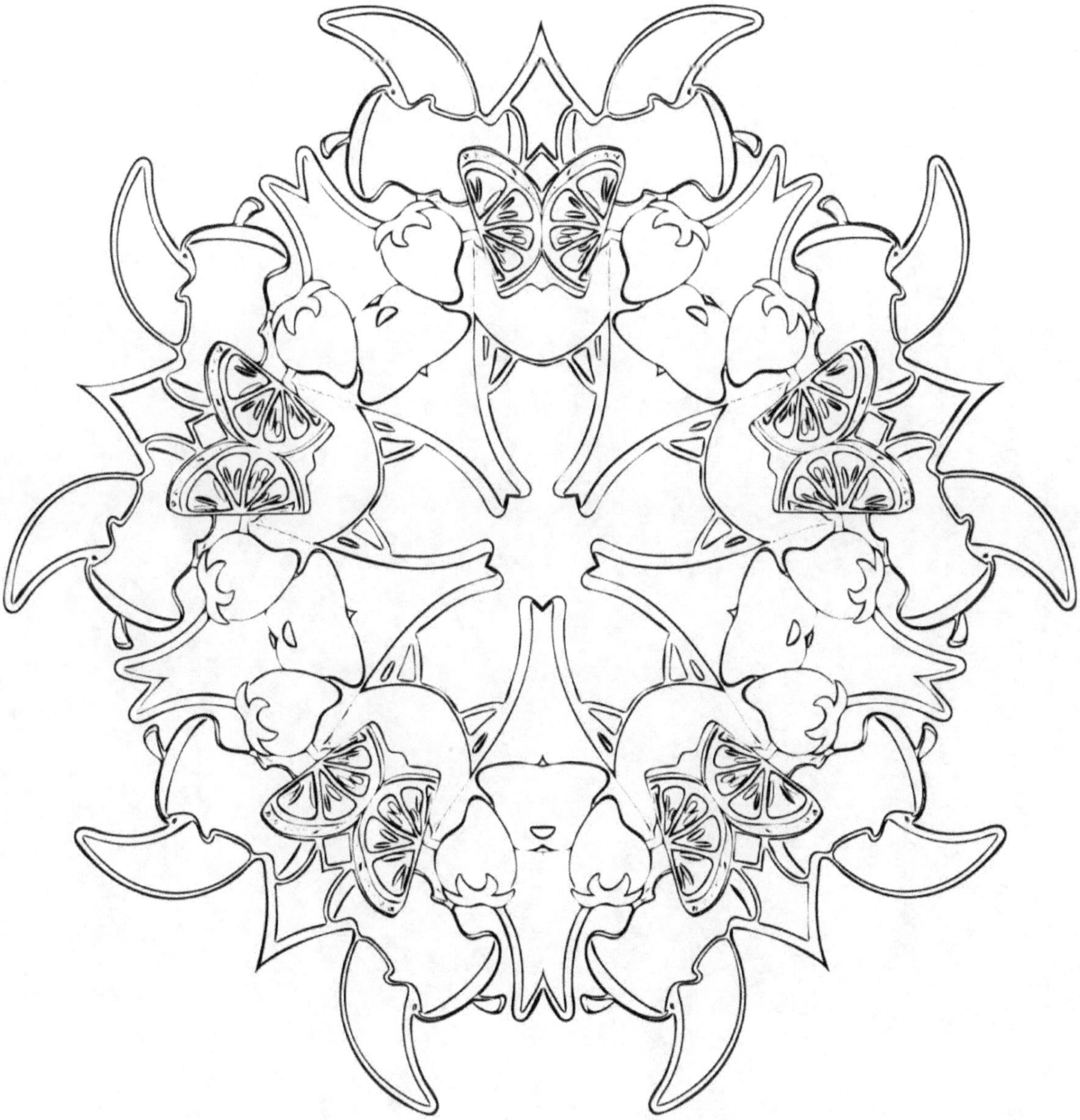

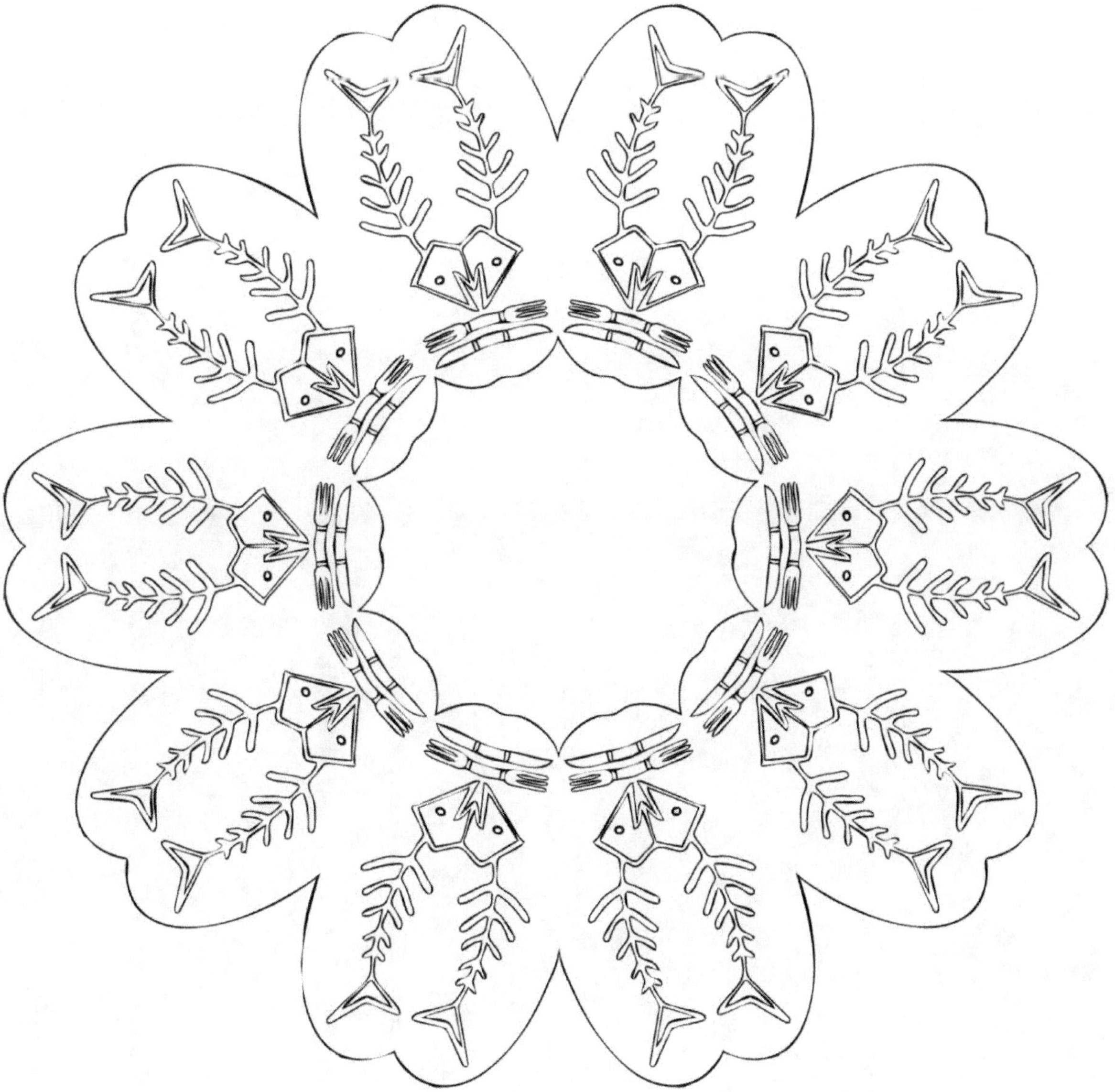

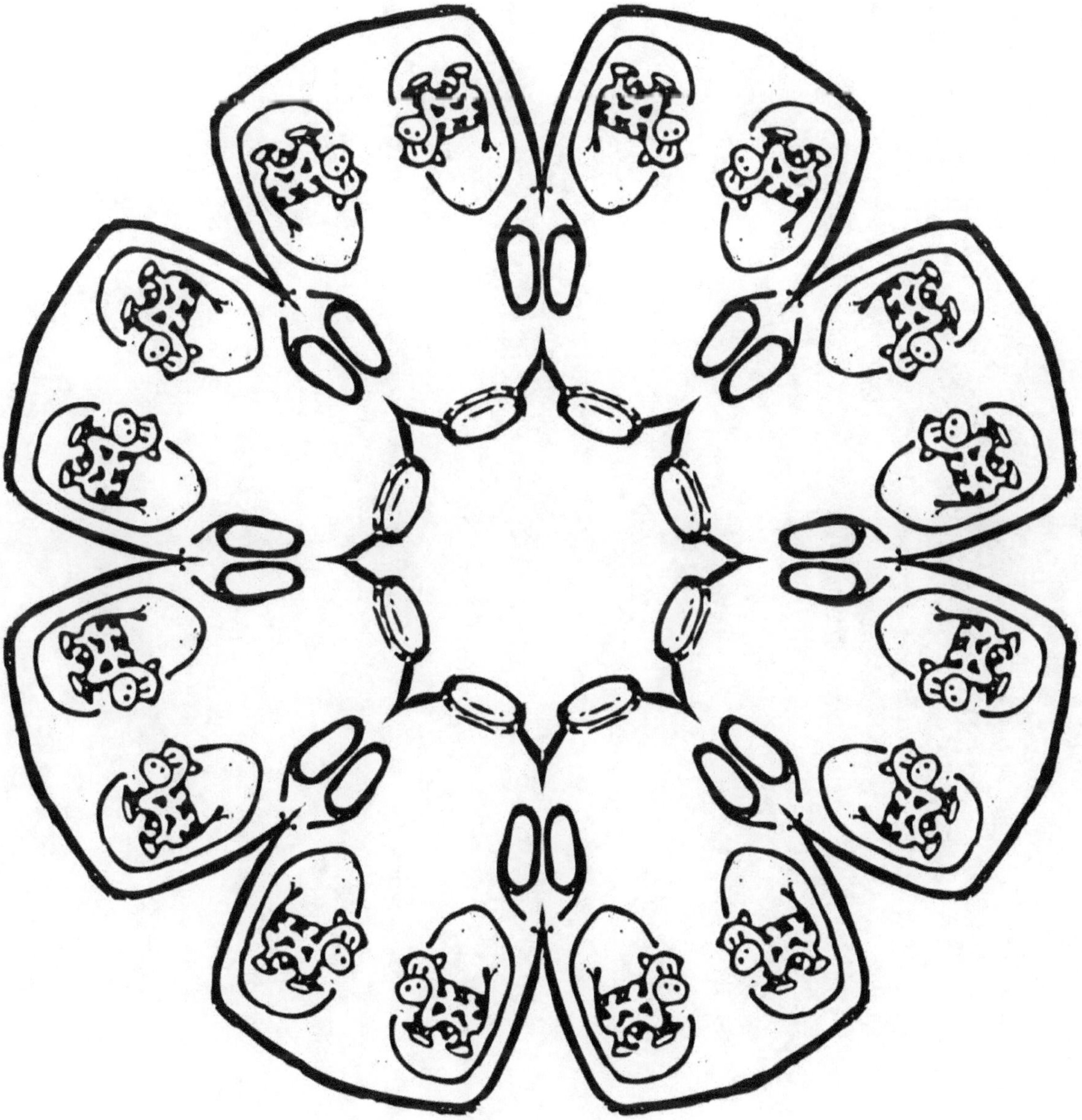

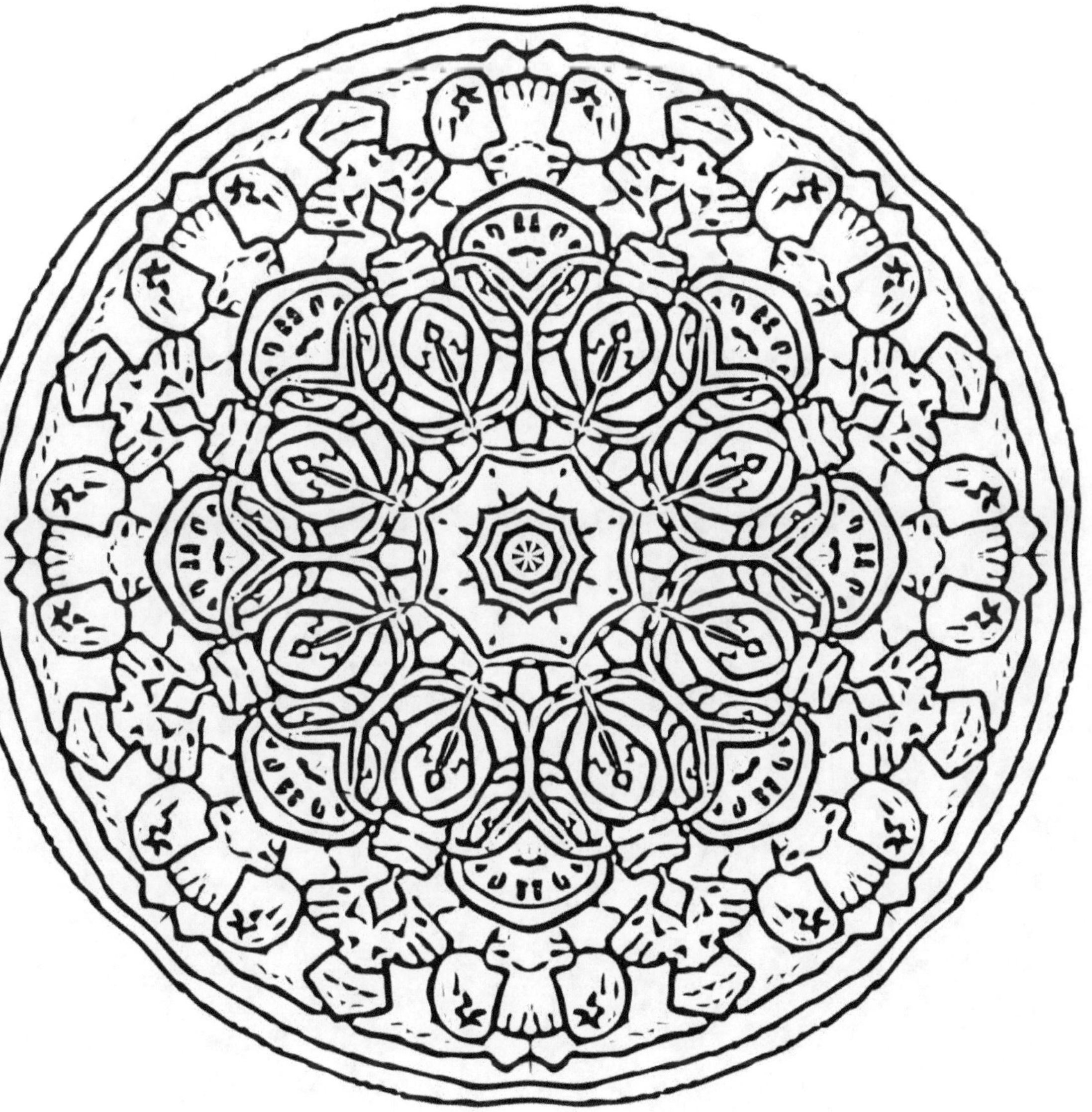

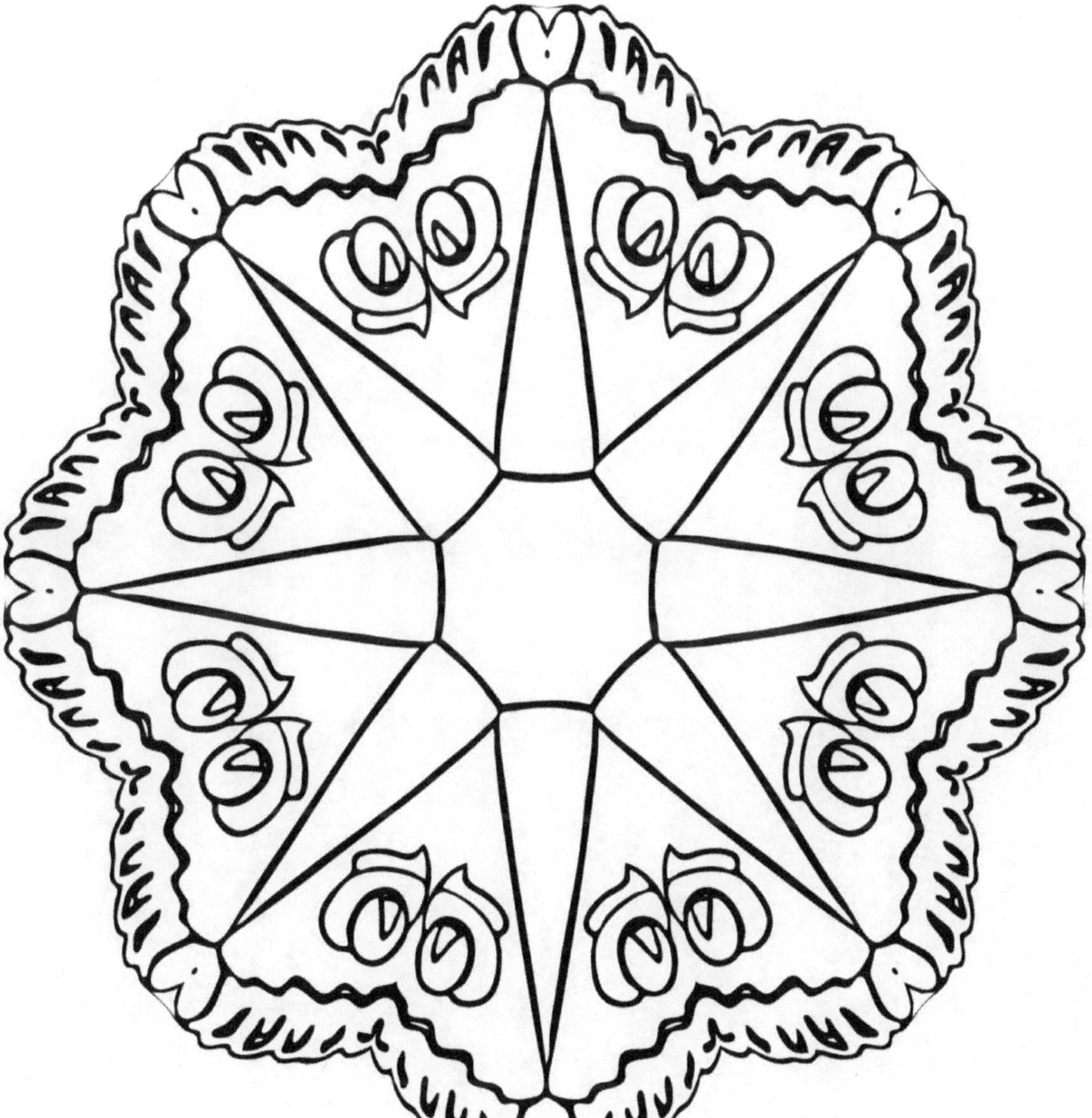

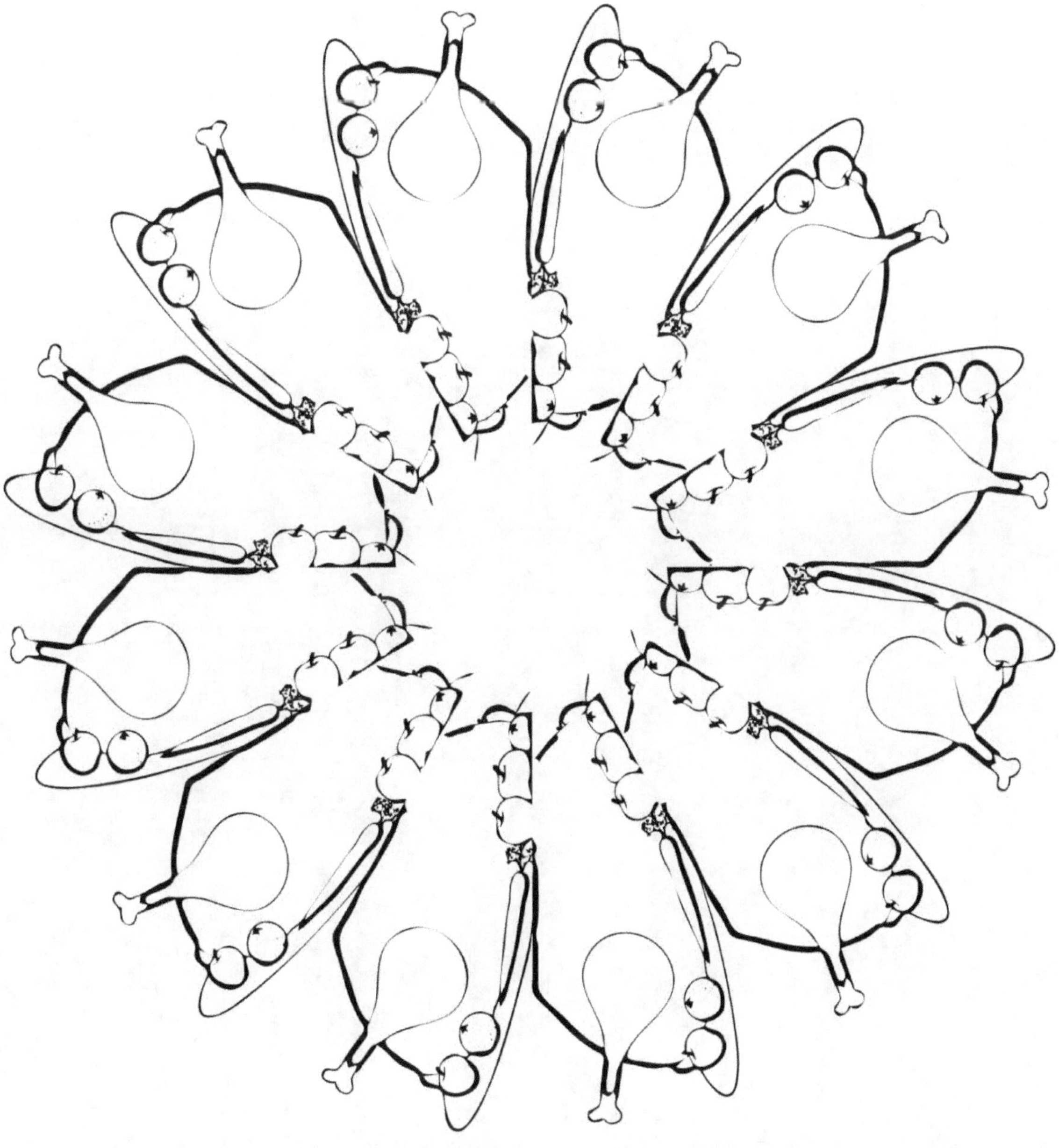

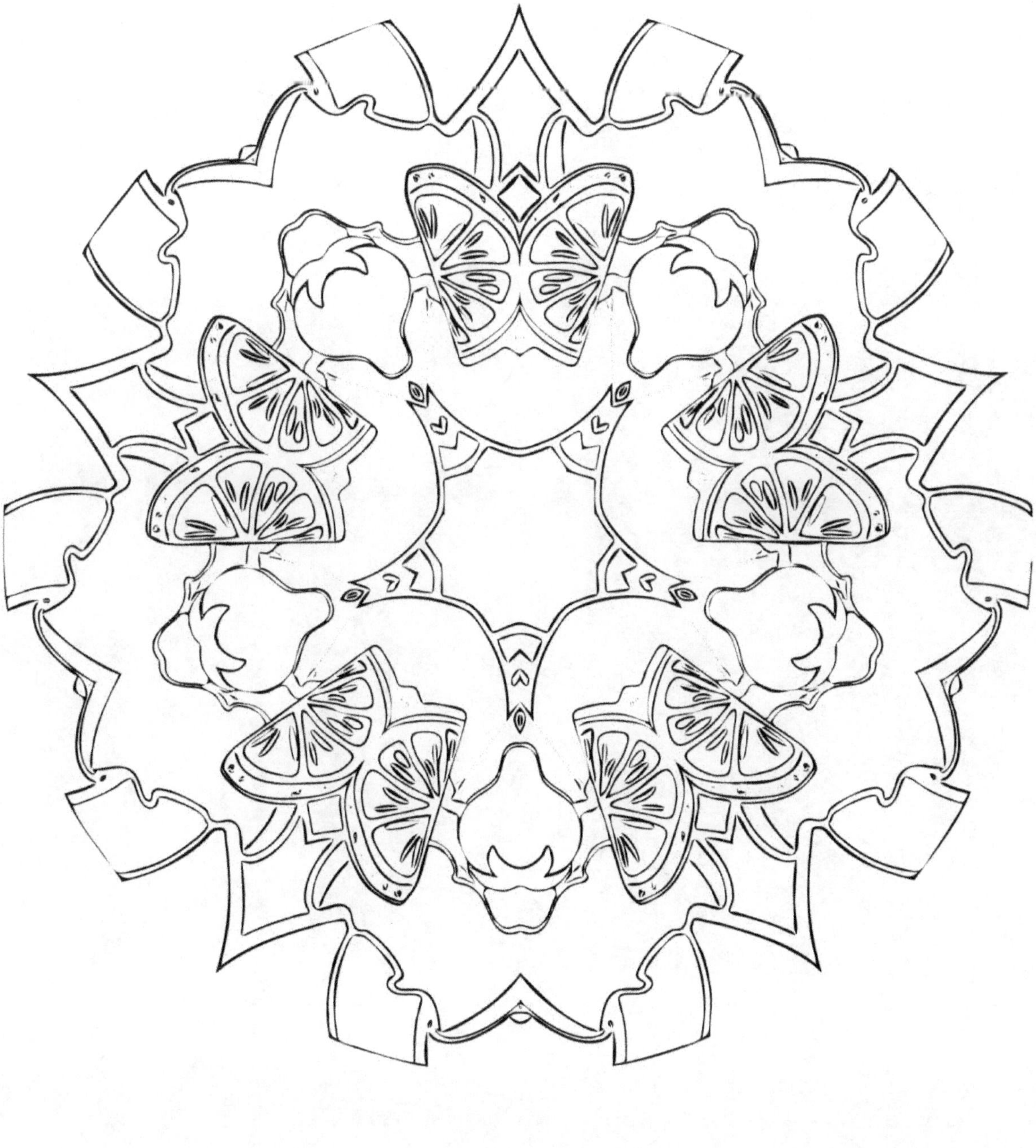

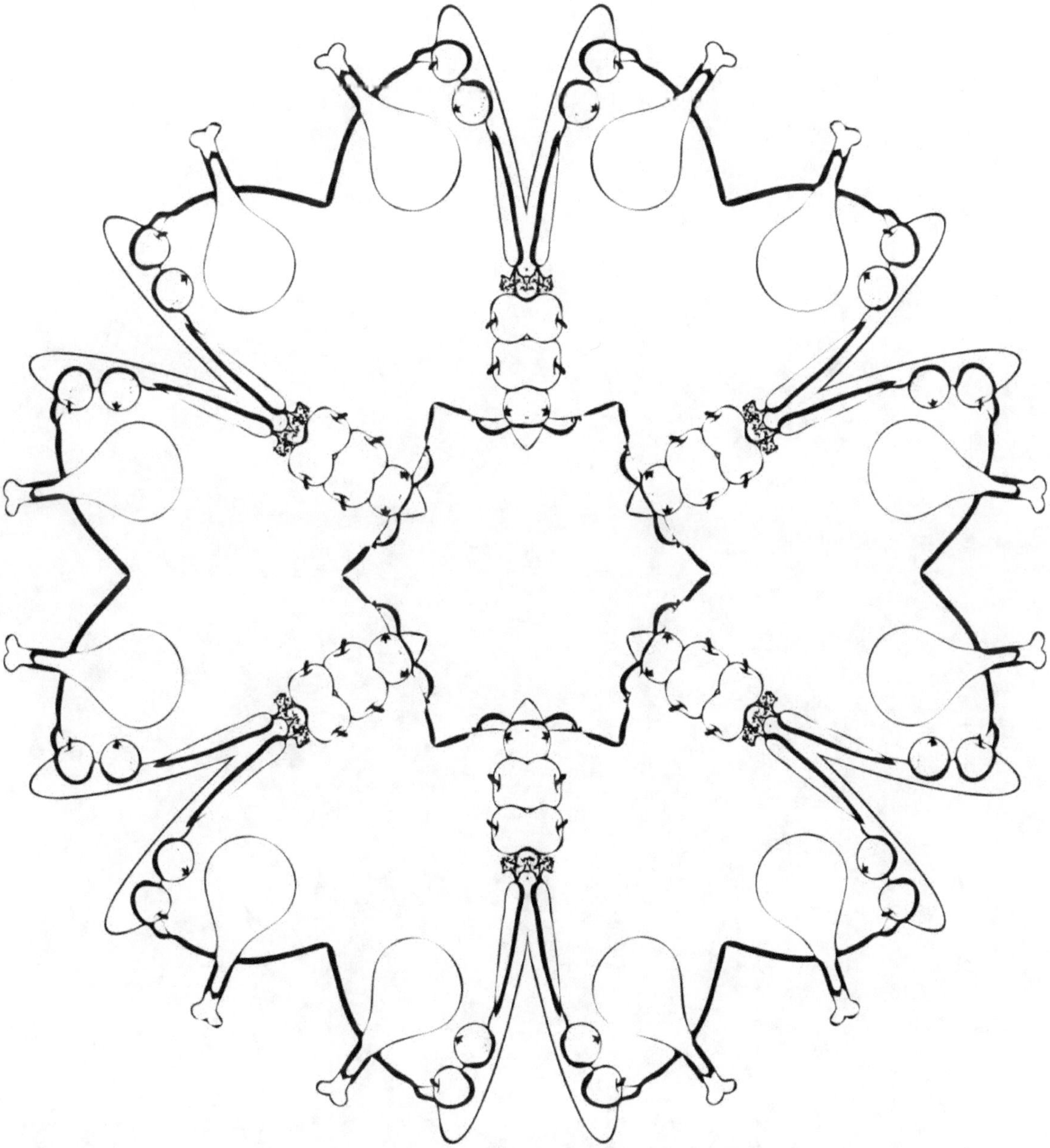

www.ingramcontent.com/pod-product-compliance
Lightning Source LLC
Chambersburg PA
CBHW080610180526
45168CB00007B/2856
* 9 7 8 1 5 1 7 7 1 2 9 8 3 *